Really WILD

LIONS

Claire Robinson

Heinemann LIBRARY

First published in Great Britain by Heinemann Library
Halley Court, Jordan Hill, Oxford, OX2 8EJ,
a division of Reed Educational and Professional Publishing Ltd

OXFORD FLORENCE PRAGUE MADRID ATHENS
MELBOURNE AUCKLAND KUALA LUMPUR SINGAPORE TOKYO
IBADAN NAIROBI KAMPALA JOHANNESBURG GABORONE
PORTSMOUTH NH (USA) CHICAGO MEXICO CITY SAO PAULO

Designed by Celia Floyd
Illustrations by Alan Fraser (Pennant Illustration) and Hardlines (map p.6)
Colour reproduction by Dot Gradations.
Printed in Hong Kong / China

01 00 99 98
10 9 8 7 6 5 4 3 2 1

ISBN 0 431 02870 2

British Library Cataloguing in Publication Data

Robinson, Claire
Lions. – (Really wild)
1. Lions – Juvenile literature
I. Title
599.7'4428

This book is also available as a hardback library edition (ISBN 0 431 03418 4)

Flick the pages of this book and see what happens!

Acknowledgements
The Publishers would like to thank the following for permission to reproduce photographs:
Bruce Coleman Ltd, p.12 (Christer Fredriksson), p.5 right (Rod Williams);
FLPA, p.7 (David Hosking), p.4 (Terry Whittaker);
NHPA/Anthony Bannister, p.5;
Oxford Scientific Films, p.21 (Jen and Des Bartlett), pp.8, 17 (David Cayless), p.10 (David
Cura), p.23 (Mark Deeble and Victoria Stone), p.16 (Gregory G. Dimijian), p.9 (John Downer),
p.19 (David Hamman), p.18 (Mike Hill), p.15 (Lee Lyon/Survival), p.22 (Sian Osolinski), p.13
(Richard Packwood), pp.14, 20 (Norbert Rosing), p.11 (Edwin Sadd), p.4 (Kjell Sanored);
Claire Robinson, p.6
Cover photograph: Oxford Scientific Films/Anthony Bannister

Our thanks to Oxford Scientific Films for their help and co-operation in the preparation of
this book.

Every effort has been made to contact copyright holders of any material reproduced in this
book. Any omissions will be rectified in subsequent printings if notice is given to the Publisher.

Contents

Some words are shown in bold, **like this**.
You can find out what they mean by
looking in the glossary.

Relatives

Lions are a type of big cat. There are 7 kinds of big cat and 29 kinds of small cat. You can see some cats here.

lion

tiger

4

caracal

desert cat

Caracals and desert cats are types of small cat.

Lions are the only cats that live in large families, or **prides**. What's it like to live in a pride of lions?

Where lions live

These lions live on the sunny **grasslands** of Africa. Zebras, giraffes, elephants and antelope live here too.

Each lion **pride** lives on its own stretch of grassland. This area of land is called a **territory**.

The pride

The largest adult males look after the **pride**. Their hairy manes make them look strong and fierce.

There are lots of females in the pride.
They care for the **cubs** and do most
of the hunting.

Sleeping

Like all cats, the lions spend most of their day resting. They love the warmth of the sun.

This **cub** is fast asleep in a tree. Look at the spotted pattern in his coat. It keeps him hidden from **predators**.

Hunting

The **pride** is hungry. The lioness **stalks** a **herd** of buffalo, keeping her head and body low in the grass.

Her sisters are ready to join her in the hunt. They work well as a team.

Eating

The **herd** panics. The lioness leaps to bring down a buffalo with her strong paws and sharp claws.

The big lions push forward to eat.
Sometimes there is not much meat left for
the **cubs**.

Rest and roar

The lions have eaten well today. They are resting. They don't need to hunt for another three or four days.

The lions see some strange male lions on their **territory**. They roar to scare them away.

Babies

One of the lionesses has given birth to **cubs**. She keeps them close by her side.

The cubs are always hungry. Their
mother lies back and feeds them with
her milk.

Growing up

The lioness keeps a close eye on her **cubs**. To move them to a safer place, she carries them gently in her mouth.

As the cubs grow up, they learn to be adult lions. They love to play fighting and hunting games.

Lion facts

- Lions have four sharp pointed **canine teeth** for killing their **prey**.

- Lions live for about 15 years.

- Lionesses give birth to a litter of **cubs**. Usually there are two or three cubs in a **litter**.

- The females in a **pride** are all related. Sometimes they feed each others' cubs.

- The females own the **territory**. The adult males live there until stronger males take their place in the pride.

- Most lions live in Africa, but there is a rare Asian lion that is only found in the Gir Forest in India.

Glossary

canine teeth   long pointed teeth

cub   baby lion

grassland   very large area of grass

herd   a large group of animals such as zebras and
antelope that live together

litter   lion cubs born at the same time

predators   animals that hunt other animals for food

prey   animal hunted as food

pride   a family, or group of lions

stalk   to follow something quietly, keeping out of sight

territory   an area of land that animals see as
their own

Index